The shep

and

the lost sheep

Jesus once told a story about a shepherd and a sheep that was lost.

One morning the shepherd came to the sheep-pen.
Inside the pen the sheep were safe from prowling lions and wolves.

The shepherd knew every one of his sheep. They belonged to him. He patted their woolly heads as they came out.

Every day he took them out to the fields to graze.
They followed him and they trusted him to keep them safe.

The sheep ate the fresh green grass while the shepherd played his flute.

But one day while they were out in the fields one of the sheep strayed away from the flock.

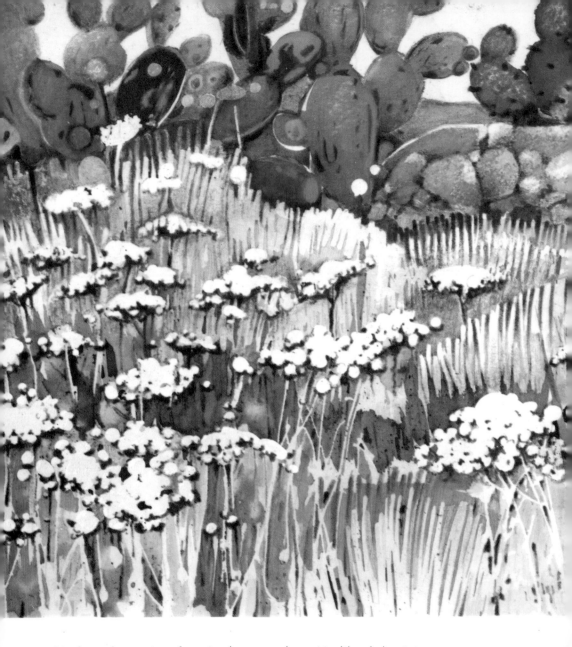

He loved running free in the meadow. He liked the juicy
green grass and the tasty shoots.

Soon he was far away from the others. He was all alone.
It was nearly night. He was lost.

That night the shepherd took his sheep back to the sheep-pen.
Every night he counted them carefully — he had a hundred sheep.

He counted them one by one — ninety-seven, ninety-eight, ninety-nine . . . there was one missing!

The shepherd left the others safe inside the pen.
Then he hurried back to look for the lost sheep. A wolf or
a lion might attack him in the dark.

The shepherd would go on looking until he found his lost sheep.
He did not care how long it took. He would search all night.

Then, in the darkness he heard the sheep bleating.
It was lost and frightened.

'At last,' said the shepherd when he saw his sheep.
He picked it up gently and carried it home.

The sheep was safe once more. The shepherd was so happy
he said, 'I shall have a party for all my friends because
I have found my lost sheep.'

Jesus said, 'God is like a shepherd. Each one of us is like the lost sheep. When he finds us and makes us safe in his care there is joy in heaven.'

The shepherd and the lost sheep

Jesus told many stories, or parables, to show us what God is like. The parable of the shepherd and the lost sheep is in the New Testament of the Bible in Matthew chapter 18 and Luke chapter 15.

This parable tells us that God looks after us as a shepherd looks after his sheep. The shepherd finds food and water for his sheep, he protects them and finds them when they are lost. In the same way God cares for us.

Jesus himself said, 'I am the good shepherd.' You can find this in John's Gospel chapter 10.

Make your own picture

Cut out the figures above. Then arrange them
on the background inside the back cover.
When you have chosen the best place for each
figure, stick them down. Now you have made your
own picture.